"When a degree of non-transferability...sufficient to make [price] discrimination profitable is present, the relation between the monopolistic seller and each buyer is, strictly, one of bilateral monopoly. The terms of the contract that will emerge between them is, therefore,...subject to the play of that 'bargaining'..." (A.C. Pigou, 1932, 278).

Price discrimination policy in the U.S. focuses mainly on intermediate good markets in which buyers have bargaining power. In fact, the primary U.S. law governing price discrimination, the Robinson-Patman Act (1936), arose from concerns that large downstream firms (e.g., chain stores) were harming smaller rivals by negotiating larger discounts with suppliers.[2] In the first formal analysis of buyer-specific price discrimination policy in intermediate good markets, Michael L. Katz (1987) examined the effects of forbidding third degree price discrimination when the bargaining power of chain stores comes from their ability to threaten credibly to integrate backward into the supply of the intermediate good. For downstream markets characterized by Cournot oligopoly, he showed that "if there is no integration under either regime [i.e., whether price discrimination is allowed or forbidden], then total output and welfare are lower when price discrimination is practiced than when it is forbidden." (Katz, Proposition 1). This is an important result for public policy toward price discrimination. Until this result, the Robinson-Patman Act had received little support[3] in the economics literature.[4]

---

[2]Although most of the Robinson-Patman claims brought by the FTC have been against sellers, it was well understood when the law was passed that the discriminating seller was often the "innocent victim" of the buyer's bargaining power. See, for example, Phillip Areeda and Louis Kaplow (1988), pp. 979-80. Congress made this recognition explicit with Section 2(f) of the Act, which makes it unlawful for a buyer "knowingly to induce or receive a discrimination in price which is prohibited by this section."

[3]It should be noted that Katz does not argue that his analysis provides support for the enforcement of the Robinson-Patman Act. However, prior to Katz's article, the Robinson-Patman Act was almost universally criticized by economists as an anticompetitive law. See, for example, Marius Schwartz (1986).

[4]Until Katz's article, the formal analysis of buyer-specific price discrimination had focused on the case of independent demands (e.g., Joan Robinson (1934), Richard Schmalensee (1981), Hal Varian (1985)). Subsequent theoretical work on third degree price discrimination has focused on discrimination by a take-it or leave-it monopolist (e.g., Marius Schwartz (1990) and David A. Malueg (1993) obtain additional results for final good markets, and Patrick DeGraba (1990) and Yoshihiro Yoshida (2000) do so for input markets.) There has been work on the effects of price discrimination in input markets under buyer-specific nonlinear contracts. See Daniel P. O'Brien and Greg Shaffer (1994). Best-customer clauses have effects that are similar to a policy against price discrimination. These clauses have been examined by Thomas Cooper and Theodore Fries (1991) for the case of linear pricing and independent demands, and by Patrick DeGraba and Andrew

The ability to pursue an outside option, such as backward integration, is an important potential source of a buyer's bargaining power, but it is not the only source. The modern literature on bargaining identifies three additional factors that may affect the relative bargaining powers of a buyer and a seller: the costs of making price concessions, the loses inflicted on each other by delaying agreement, and bargaining costs. Other factors equal, a buyer's bargaining power is greater the higher the cost it bears from granting a small price concession to the seller, the greater the loss it inflicts on the seller by delaying agreement, and the less costly it is to hold out for a better deal. Once these additional sources of bargaining power are recognized, the analysis of price discrimination is more complex than it is in the take-it or leave-it environment studied by Katz. Even if an explicit threat to integrate backward is not credible, the chain may receive a discount if it has greater bargaining power than the independent. Moreover, a policy forbidding price discrimination may do more than simply constrain the prices the seller can set; it may alter relative bargaining powers.

In this paper, I extend Katz's take-it or leave-it model to a Nash bargaining framework that incorporates four sources of bargaining power: outside options, concession costs, inflicted losses, and bargaining costs. Intermediate prices are negotiated in pair-wise meetings between the supplier and individual downstream firms, one of which (the chain store) has lower costs of integrating backward into the supply of the input. As in Katz's model, the chain's integration advantage may allow it to negotiate lower prices than its rival. However, the bargaining model provides three plausible explanations for chain discounts. First, the chain may be able to threaten credibly to integrate backward, as in Katz's model. Second, the chain may earn higher profits than its rival if it fails to reach an agreement with the supplier. In bargaining language, the chain may have a higher disagreement profit than the

---

Postlewaite (1992), R. Preston McAfee and Marius Schwartz (1994), and DeGraba (1996) for the case of nonlinear pricing in intermediate good markets.

rival, which gives it greater bargaining power. Third, the chain may have lower bargaining costs than the rival. For example, the chain may have a lower discount rate than the rival, which makes it less costly for the chain to hold out for a better deal.[5]

I find that the effects of forbidding price discrimination depend crucially on the credibility of chain's threat to integrate backward. If the integration threat is a binding outside option, then Katz's results are unchanged; forbidding price discrimination reduces the average wholesale price if the chain chooses not to integrate in both regimes. However, if the integration threat is not a binding outside option, then forbidding price discrimination raises the average wholesale price for a wide range of parameters that determine relative bargaining powers. Thus, when bargaining power comes from sources other than outside options, the results of the take-it or leave-it model are often reversed.

An important difference between the bargaining and take-it or leave-it environments is that in the former, forbidding price discrimination alters the firms' relative costs of making price concessions, which affects their relative bargaining powers. When price discrimination is allowed, a buyer's price concession (an agreement to pay a higher price) weakens its competitive position in the downstream market relative to rivals that do not make the same concession. When discrimination is forbidden, however, a buyer's concession does not weaken its competitive position (though it reduces its profits), because the higher price must be paid by every firm that purchases the product from the supplier. Therefore, the cost of a price concession is lower for a buyer when price discrimination is forbidden than when it is allowed. On the other hand, it is more costly for the seller to make a price concession (an agreement to accept a lower price) when price discrimination is forbidden, because a lower price must then be given to every downstream firm. Under both concession cost effects, a policy forbidding

---

[5]A fourth source of countervailing power identified in the literature is the ability of buyers to accumulate a backlog of unfilled orders that, similar to a boom in demand, forces sellers to collude on low prices to prevent undercutting (Christopher M. Snyder, 1996). This source of bargaining power does not arise in my model, which focuses on the behavior of a single upstream firm.

price discrimination reduces the bargaining power of downstream firms relative to the seller.

The implications of the concession cost effect of price discrimination policy are clearest when downstream firms have equal bargaining power and the chain cannot credibly threaten to integrate backward when price discrimination is allowed. In this case, a policy forbidding price discrimination raises the wholesale price charged to *both* downstream firms, reducing total output and welfare. Critics of price discrimination policy have often argued that the effects of forbidding price discrimination reach beyond markets exhibiting persistent asymmetries in input prices. A common criticism is that forbidding price discrimination prevents sporadic and selective discounts by cartel members that might break down cartel discipline and lead to lower prices.[6] My results show that upstream competition is not necessary for a policy forbidding price discrimination to raise prices in markets where systematic discrimination is not observed. All that is required is buyer bargaining power.

If the chain has greater bargaining power than the rival, then the analysis is less clear cut. The key complication is that when price discrimination is forbidden, the supplier prefers to have the weaker buyer negotiate the common price, while the buyers both prefer to have the stronger buyer negotiate the price. I show that if the supplier negotiates with the weaker buyer, and if the chain's integration threat does not bind when discrimination is allowed, then a policy forbidding price discrimination raises the average wholesale price. On the other hand, if the buyers can arrange to have the stronger buyer negotiate price, forbidding price discrimination can reduce the average price if the discounts received by the stronger buyer when discrimination is allowed are large enough.

The remainder of this paper is organized as follows. The bargaining model is introduced in Section I. Section II presents the implications of the bargaining model when price discrimination is allowed. Section III examines the effects of forbidding price discrimination.

---

[6]See, e.g., Dennis W. Carlton and Jeffrey M. Perloff (1994), p. 416.

Section IV examines two special cases of the model: independent demands, and "almost competitive" conduct in the downstream market. Section V concludes the paper. Technical proofs are presented in the Appendix.

I.   A Bargaining Model of Third Degree Price Discrimination

To facilitate comparison with Katz, I adopt a similar framework with some additional notation required to account for bargaining. There is a monopoly supplier of an input used by two downstream firms to produce a final product. The downstream firms are engaged in rivalry summarized by their reduced form profit functions. Let $\pi_1(w_1, w_2)$ and $\pi_2(w_1, w_2)$ be the equilibrium profits of downstream firms 1 and 2, respectively, when their wholesale prices are w_1 and w_2 (the negotiations determining w_1 and w_2 are detailed below). The supplier's reduced form profit is $U(w_1, w_2)$. I assume that the profit functions have the usual properties, i.e., $\partial \pi_i / \partial w_i < 0$, $0 \leq \partial \pi_i / \partial w_j < |\partial \pi_i / w_i|$, and $\partial U / \partial w_i > 0$ up to some maximum for $i \in \{1, 2\}$, $i \neq j$. I also assume that downstream rivalry (but not bargaining power) is symmetric in the sense that $\pi_1(w, w') = \pi_2(w', w)$ and $U(w, w') = U(w', w)$ for all w, w'.

Downstream firm 1 (the "chain store") has the option of integrating backward into the supply of the input. If the chain integrates backward, it incurs a fixed cost F and pays a wholesale price v. Its profits are then $\pi^I(v, w_2) = \pi_1(v, w_2) - F$, firm 2's profits are $\pi_2(v, w_2)$, and the upstream firm's profits are $U(v, w_2)$ if price discrimination is allowed and $U^F(v, w_2) \leq U(v, w_2)$ if price discrimination is forbidden.[7] Downstream firm 2 (the "independent") cannot integrate backward.[8]

---

[7]If the chain integrates backward and price discrimination is allowed, the supplier can win the right to supply it by offering to sell at (or just below) v. If price discrimination is forbidden, the supplier's profit U^F is the maximum of the profit earned from selling to both firms at v or only to the independent at w_2.

[8]The chain's integration profits π^I can also be interpreted as its profits after spending the fixed cost F to purchase from an alternative supplier at a wholesale price of v. One motivation for the chain's superior outside opportunities is that it operates in more markets than the independent and spreads the fixed costs

Following Ken Binmore et al. (1986), I model negotiations using an asymmetric Nash bargaining framework and motivate the role of outside options, disagreement payoffs, and bargaining weights from an underlying noncooperative bargaining game.[9] When price discrimination is allowed, the supplier attempts to negotiate a separate wholesale price with each downstream firm. Suppose the supplier and firm 2 have agreed (or are expected to agree) to the price w_2 (the negotiations determining w_2 will be described shortly). In an equilibrium in which the chain chooses not to integrate backward, the asymmetric Nash bargaining solution between the supplier and the chain solves

$$(1) \quad \max_{w_1} \phi_1(w_1, w_2) = [U(w_1, w_2) - d_{u1}]^{1-\gamma_1} [\pi(w_1, w_2) - d_1]^{\gamma_1} \ s.t. \ \pi_1(w_1, w_2) \geq \pi^I(v, w_2^I)$$

where d_{u1} and d_1 are the disagreement payoffs of the supplier and the chain, respectively; w_2^I is the wholesale price that the independent would pay if the chain were to integrate backward; and γ_1 is the chain's bargaining weight in negotiations with the supplier.[10] These parameters are explained as follows.

The bargaining weight γ_1 can be motivated from an alternating-offer bargaining model (Rubinstein, 1982) that underlies the Nash bargaining solution, as demonstrated in Binmore et al. (1986). In this class of models, firms are motivated to reach agreement by the cost of bargaining delays. In one variant (the *time preference Nash solution*), delays are costly because firms discount the future at positive rates. In the other variant (the *standard Nash solution*), delays are costly because there is an exogenous risk that negotiations might break down after each period in which the firms fail to reach an agreement. Both motivations may play a role in negotiations over intermediate good prices, since firms generally discount the future at positive rates and there is often some risk that a profitable opportunity will be

---

of obtaining alternative supplies over greater sales.

[9]This approach to modelling negotiations is consistent with what Binmore and Partha Dasgupta (1987) call the "Nash program," which seeks to motivate cooperative approaches to the bargaining problem like the Nash bargaining solution from an underlying noncooperative game.

[10]The individual rationality constraints, $U \geq d_{u1}$ and $\pi_1 \geq d_1$, are omitted for brevity.

exploited by a third party. Binmore et al. show that the unique subgame perfect equilibrium to the Rubinstein bargaining game converges to an asymmetric Nash bargaining solution as the time between offers becomes small. Each firm's bargaining weight in this solution is a decreasing function of its bargaining cost, as measured by its discount rate.[11] Intuitively, the more costly it is for a firm to reject an offer, the less bargaining power the firm has. This is reflected by a lower bargaining weight in the asymmetric Nash bargaining solution.

The disagreement payoffs can also be motivated from the same Rubinstein-style bargaining model that yields the bargaining weights. Binmore et al. show that in the time preference solution, the disagreement payoffs are the profits earned by firms while they are negotiating prices. In the standard solution, the disagreement payoffs are the profits received if negotiations break down.[12] I assume that the disagreement profits are small enough that there exists a set $\mathcal{A}$ of wholesale prices such that $U(w_1, w_2) > d_{ui}$ and $\pi_i(w_1, w_2) > d_i$ for all $(w_1, w_2) \in \mathcal{A}$, $i \in \{1, 2\}$.

The constraint in the maximization problem reflects the "outside option principle" (Avner Shaked and John Sutton, 1984). Binmore et al. showed that when the Nash bargaining solution is motivated from an alternating-offer bargaining game, an outside option should be modelled as a constraint on the equilibrium prices, separately from the disagreement payoffs. The outside option affects the bargaining solution only if the solution to the bargaining

---

[11]Specifically, suppose the one-period discount rates of firm i and the upstream supplier are r_i and r_u, respectively. In the time preference solution, where there is no probability that negotiations will terminate in a breakdown, Binmore et al. show that the subgame perfect equilibrium to the Rubinstein game converges to an asymmetric Nash bargaining solution in which firm i's bargaining weight is $\gamma_i = r_i/(r_i + r_u)$. Suppose instead that firms do not discount the future, but that there is an exogenous probability α_i that negotiations between the supplier and firm i will break down after any period that one of them rejects the other's offer. In this case, Binmore et al. show that the alternating-offer bargaining game between the supplier and firm i converges to the (symmetric) Nash bargaining solution. Abhinay Muthoo (1999) considers an alternating offer bargaining model in which both types of delay costs (discounting and the risk of a breakdown) are present. His results imply that firm i's bargaining weight in this case is $\gamma_i = (r_i + \alpha_i)/(2\alpha_i + r_i + r_u)$.

[12]Let $\overline{U}_i$ and $\overline{\pi}_i$ be the profits earned by the supplier and firm i, respectively, each period *during* their negotiations; let b_{ui} and b_i be their profits (per period) in the event negotiations break down. When both motivations for reaching agreement are present, the results of Muthoo (1999) imply that the disagreement profits are $d_{ui} = (\overline{U}_i + \alpha_i b_u)/(r_u + \alpha_i)$ and $d_i = (\overline{\pi}_i + \alpha_i b_i)/(r_i + \alpha_i)$.

game ignoring the outside option yields a lower payoff to the chain than it would receive by exercising its option. If the chain chooses integration, I assume that the supplier and firm 2 negotiate (or renegotiate) their price. This leads to a wholesale price for firm 2 of w_2^I. I assume that there exists a set $\mathcal{A}_1$ of wholesale prices for firm 1 such that $U(w_1, w_2^I) > d_{ui}$ for all $w_1 \in \mathcal{A}_1$, $i \in \{1, 2\}$.

The wholesale price negotiated by the supplier and firm 2 solves a similar Nash bargaining problem without the integration constraint:

$$(2) \qquad \max_{w_2} \quad \phi_2(w_1, w_2) = [U(w_1, w_2) - d_{u2}]^{1-\gamma_2}[\pi_2(w_1, w_2) - d_2]^{\gamma_2}$$

where d_{u2} and d_2 are the disagreement payoffs of the supplier and firm 2, and γ_2 is firm 2's bargaining weight.[13] These parameters are interpreted the same way as the analogous parameters in negotiations with the chain.

The first order conditions for (1) and (2) are

$$(3) \qquad (1-\gamma_1)\frac{\partial U}{\partial w_1}[\pi_1 - d_1] + \gamma_1\frac{\partial \pi_1}{\partial w_1}[U - d_{u1}] + \lambda\frac{\partial \pi_1}{\partial w_1} = 0,$$

$$(4) \qquad \lambda \geq 0, \quad \lambda[\pi_1 - \pi^I] = 0;$$

$$(5) \qquad (1-\gamma_2)\frac{\partial U}{\partial w_2}[\pi_2 - d_2] + \gamma_2\frac{\partial \pi_2}{\partial w_2}[U - d_{u2}] = 0$$

where λ is a Lagrangian multiplier. The solution to conditions (3) and (4) defines a "bargaining reaction function," $R_1(w_2)$, which expresses the wholesale price negotiated by the manufacturer and firm 1 as a function of the wholesale price negotiated with firm 2. The bargaining reaction function for firm 2, $R_2(w_1)$, is defined symmetrically as the solution to (5). A bargaining equilibrium when price discrimination is allowed is a pair of wholesale prices (w_1^A, w_2^A) (the superscript 'A' for "allowed") such that $w_1^A = R_1(w_2^A)$ and $w_2^A = R_2(w_1^A)$.

I make the following additional assumptions:

---

[13]Note that I am ignoring the possibility that firm 2 might want to choose a wholesale price that would induce chain integration. This possibility is ruled out by Assumption 4 below.

Assumption 1 $U(w_1, w_2)$ *is strictly quasi-concave.*

Assumption 2 $\phi_i(w_1, w_2)$ *is strictly quasi-concave in* w_i, $i \in \{1, 2\}$.

Assumption 3 $\phi_i(w, w)$ *is strictly quasi-concave in* w, $i \in \{1, 2\}$.

Assumption 4 $-1 < R'_i(w_j) \leq (\partial \pi_i / \partial w_j)/(\partial \pi_i / \partial w_i)$, $i \in \{1, 2\}$, $i \neq j$.

Assumptions 1–3 imply that the supplier's profit function and the Nash products with and without price discrimination are single-peaked. Assumption 4 embodies two assumptions. The second inequality is true if and only if firm i's profits from its negotiations with the supplier are increasing in firm j's wholesale price. This assumption is quite natural, although it is not implied by the others. Combining this assumption with the first inequality in Assumption 4 ensures that the bargaining equilibrium is (locally) strictly stable. These assumptions are satisfied in a variety of environments, e.g., under Cournot or differentiated Bertrand competition with linear demand and constant marginal cost.

II. Price Discrimination in the Bargaining Model

A. Equilibrium When Price Discrimination is Allowed

Intuition about the bargaining solution can be gained by rewriting the first order condition for the negotiations between the supplier and firm i when the integration constraint is slack:

$$(6) \qquad \frac{\gamma_i[-\partial \pi_i(w_1^A, w_2^A)/\partial w_i]}{\pi_i(w_1^A, w_2^A) - d_i} = \frac{(1 - \gamma_i)[\partial U(w_1^A, w_2^A)/\partial w_i]}{U(w_1^A, w_2^A) - d_{ui}}$$

or

$$(7) \qquad \frac{\text{Firm } i\text{'s weighted concession cost}}{\text{Firm } i\text{'s net profits}} = \frac{\text{Supplier's weighted concession cost}}{\text{Supplier's net profits}}.$$

That is, in a bargaining equilibrium, the wholesale price negotiated by the supplier and firm i equalizes their weighted concession costs as a percentage of their gains from trade, where

9

the weights are the firms' bargaining weights. The intuitive interpretation of this condition is that the firm with the lower percentage concession cost loses less when improving its offer and thus should do so to facilitate reaching agreement.[14] Note that π_i is decreasing and U is increasing in w_i over the range of conflict relevant for bargaining. Using this fact, it is straightforward to see the effects of different sources of firm i's bargaining power from condition (6). Other factors equal, an increase in firm i's (absolute) concession costs $(-\partial \pi_i / \partial w_i)$ requires an increase in firm i's relative profits for condition (6) to continue to hold. This requires a reduction in firm i's wholesale price. Similarly, an increase in firm i's bargaining weight, an increase in its disagreement profit, or a decrease in the supplier's disagreement profit will result in a decrease in firm i's wholesale price for any given w_j.

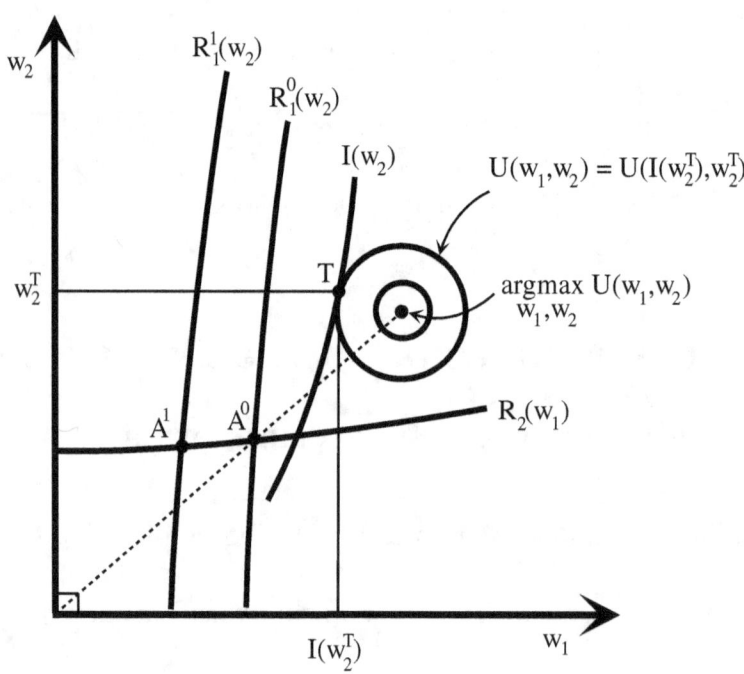

Figure 1: Bargaining equilibrium when price discrimination is allowed.

The equilibrium prices are illustrated in Figure 1, which is analogous to Figure 1 in Katz. The curve $I(w_2)$ represents the value of w_1 such that the chain is indifferent be-

---

[14]This heuristic is due to Frederik Zeuthen (1930), who described this solution for the case of equal bargaining weights. John Harsanyi (1956) demonstrates that Zeuthen's heuristic solution is equivalent to the symmetric Nash bargaining solution.

tween integration and non-integration when the wholesale prices are $I(w_2)$ and w_2, i.e., $\pi_1(I(w_2), w_2) = \pi^I(v, w_2)$ for all w_2. The chain prefers integration over non-integration for all (w_1, w_2) to the right of $I(w_2)$. The integration constraint was the only source of chain bargaining power in the take-it or leave-it model studied by Katz. He showed that if the supplier finds it profitable to sell to the chain, it maximizes profits by choosing the whole-sale prices represented by point T, where the supplier's iso-profit contour is tangent to the integration constraint. The chain receives a discount relative to the independent because it has a credible threat to integrate backward.

In the bargaining model, the integration constraint will not bind if the chain has enough bargaining power from other sources. For example, point A^0 represents a bargaining equilibrium when downstream firms have symmetric bargaining power ($d_1 = d_2$, $d_{u1} = d_{u2}$, $\gamma_1 = \gamma_2$) high enough that the integration constraint is slack. An increase in the chain's bargaining power through any of the mechanisms described above is represented as a leftward shift of its bargaining reaction function, e.g., from $R_1^0(w_2)$ to $R_1^1(w_2)$. This changes equilibrium wholesale prices from point A^0 to point A^1. The chain's wholesale price falls unambiguously. The independent's price may rise or fall, but Assumption 4 implies that it cannot fall by more than the chain's price. Thus, an increase in the chain's bargaining power allows it to negotiate a discount relative to the independent. These results are summarized in the following Lemma.

Lemma 1 *Suppose the integration constraint is slack. Then in a bargaining equilibrium when price discrimination is allowed, firm i's wholesale price w_i^A is strictly decreasing in γ_i, d_i, and $-d_{ui}$. Moreover, firm i's equilibrium discount, $w_j^A - w_i^A$, is strictly increasing in γ_i, d_i, and $-d_{ui}$.*

B. How Bargaining Can Lead to Chain Discounts

When Robinson-Patman was passed, the common perception was that chain stores tended to pay lower wholesale prices than independents. In this model, four types of factors affect the chain's ability to negotiate discounts: the chain's integration threat, the buyers' disagreement profits, the supplier's disagreement profits, and the firms' bargaining weights. I discuss briefly the role each factor might play in generating chain discounts.

The potential for backward integration (or, more generally, the ability to seek alternative supplies) affects the chain's bargaining power by giving it an outside option. The effect of this option is similar to its role in the take-it or leave-it model studied by Katz. In both cases, the potential for backward integration may constrain the wholesale prices the supplier can charge without inducing chain integration. The main difference between the models is that the threat to integrate backward is not a binding constraint in the bargaining model if the chain has enough bargaining power from other sources.

From Lemma 1, a sufficient condition for the chain to receive a discount is that $d_1 \geq d_2$, $d_{u1} \leq d_{u2}$, and $\gamma_1 \geq \gamma_2$, with at least one of these inequalities being strict. Consider first the disagreement profits of the downstream firms. The chain's disagreement profit will exceed the independent's if the chain has a more profitable "inside option," i.e., if it earns greater profits than the independent *during* its negotiations with the supplier.[15] For example, the chain may be able to substitute another product during negotiations that achieves greater sales or a higher margin than the independent could achieve with its next best alternative. The chain's disagreement profit will also exceed the independent's if it earns greater profit in the event negotiations break down. For example, suppose the exogenous risk of a breakdown arises from the possibility of new entry that would make it unprofitable for the downstream firms

---

[15]Muthoo (1999) refers to the profit earned by a player during negotiations as its "inside option."

12

to carry the supplier's product. If the chain has better alternatives than the independent, then $d_1 > d_2$.

The chain can also receive a discount if, other factors equal, the supplier's disagreement profit in negotiations with the chain is lower than its disagreement profit in negotiations with the independent, i.e., $d_{u1} < d_{u2}$. Suppose that if negotiations break down with the chain, but not the independent, the chain will be a stronger competitor against the independent than the independent would be against the chain in the opposite situation where negotiations broke down with only the independent.[16] If the chain integration constraint is slack in the event negotiations break down with the independent, we would expect $d_{u1} < d_{u2}$. The logic is that if the supplier is unconstrained in selling to only one of the downstream firms, it is better off selling unconstrained to the firm that faces less vigourous competition.[17]

Finally, the chain will also receive a discount if, other factors equal, it has a greater bargaining weight than the independent. This occurs if the chain has a lower discount rate, which might be the case if it has lower capital costs than the independent.

III.   The Effects of Forbidding Price Discrimination

When price discrimination is forbidden, the two buyers will pay a single price.[18] It is not obvious what role each firm will play in determining that price. One possibility is that the supplier can select one of the downstream firms to negotiate a common price. At an intuitive

---

[16]A breakdown with only one of the downstream firms might occur if an entrant comes in and displaces only that firm.

[17]Plausible reasons can also be given for why d_{u1} might exceed d_{u2}. For example, if the chain integration constraint binds in the event negotiations with the independent break down, then the supplier might earn more selling through the independent than the chain if the chain has better outside opportunities than the independent. As another example, suppose the supplier's inside option in negotiations with firm i is the profit it earns from sales to firm j while it negotiates with firm i. If the price charged to independent during negotiations with the chain is higher than the price charged the chain during negotiations with the independent in this event, then it is also possible to have $d_{u1} > d_{u2}$.

[18]In this paper I am abstracting from enforcement costs that might permit some price discrimination to go unchallenged even when discrimination is illegal.

level, one might argue that even if the other downstream firm would like to participate in the bargaining, the supplier does not have to listen to the other firm while it negotiates with the firm it selects. On the other hand, the downstream firms have a joint incentive to have the stronger firm negotiate price because both benefit from having a lower, common marginal cost. If the downstream firms can coordinate their strategies, the weaker firm may simply refuse to listen to the supplier, thinking that its rival may be able to negotiate a lower price.

Another issue when price discrimination is forbidden is whether the first buyer to reach agreement determines the wholesale price for the second, or whether the second buyer can negotiate a new price that must then be given to first. The answer to this question is likely to depend on the nature of supplier and buyer liability under the rule that prohibits price discrimination. For example, suppose the supplier first negotiates a "high" wholesale price with the independent. The chain might then try to negotiate a lower price. However, if the supplier keeps the high price in place with the independent, then the chain may risk being sued by the independent and the authority that enforces the rule against price discrimination. As noted in footnote 2, the chain would be liable under Section 2(f) of the Robinson-Patman Act. The supplier would also be liable under the other Sections of the Act, but if a lawsuit would result in a cease and desist order that would allow the supplier to charge both buyers the high price, then price discrimination may be worth the risk. If this were true, the chain would be better off simply accepting the high price or pursuing its outside option. On the other hand, if the supplier's liability is sufficiently high, or if a cease and desist order would lead to the low price for both buyers, then the supplier may accede to the chain's demands. A third possibility is that the supplier would simply refuse to sell to the chain unless it agreed to the same price as the independent. If this were credible, the chain would presumably agree to the higher price or exercise its outside option.

In this paper, I will not attempt to resolve the buyer coordination and legal liability questions that affect the influence each buyer is likely to have in negotiating a common price. Instead, I will consider two cases distinguished by which buyer negotiates the wholesale price. These two cases represent endpoints of the set of agreements that are likely to emerge from bargaining when price discrimination is forbidden.

Suppose first that the supplier negotiates a common price with the independent. If both firms prefer to have the chain remain non-integrated, their Nash bargaining solution solves

$$\max_{w} \; \phi_2(w,w) = [U(w,w) - d_{u2}]^{1-\gamma_2}[\pi_2(w,w) - d_2]^{\gamma_2} \;\; s.t. \; \pi_1(w,w) \geq \pi^I(v,w_2^I).$$

The first order condition is

$$
\begin{aligned}
0 &= (1-\gamma_2)\sum_i \frac{\partial U}{\partial w_i}[\pi_2 - d_2] + \gamma_2 \sum_i \frac{\partial \pi_2}{\partial w_i}[U - d_{u2}] + \eta \sum_i \frac{\partial \pi_1}{\partial w_i} \\
\text{(8)} \quad &= \frac{\partial \phi_2}{\partial w_2} + \left\{ (1-\gamma_2)\frac{\partial U}{\partial w_1}[\pi_2 - d_2] + \gamma_2 \frac{\partial \pi_2}{\partial w_1}[U - d_{u2}] \right\} + \eta \sum_i \frac{\partial \pi_1}{\partial w_i},
\end{aligned}
$$

$$\text{(9)} \qquad\qquad \eta \geq 0, \quad \eta[\pi_2(w,w) - \pi^I(v,w_2^I)] = 0$$

where η is a Lagrangian multiplier. Recall that $\partial \phi_2/\partial w_2$ is the derivative of the Nash product for negotiations between the supplier and firm 2 when discrimination is allowed. Suppose first that firms 1 and 2 are symmetric except for their abilities to integrate backward (i.e., $d_1 = d_2$, $d_{u1} = d_{u2}$, and $\gamma_1 = \gamma_2$). Then $w_1^A = w_2^A$, and $\partial \phi_2(w_2^A, w_2^A)/\partial w_2 = 0$ by the first order condition for the optimal choice of w_2^A. The term in curly braces in (8) is positive at (w_1^A, w_2^A) because firm 2's profit is increasing in w_1, $\partial U/\partial w_1$ is positive over the range of conflict, and net profits are positive in a bargaining equilibrium when discrimination is allowed. Therefore, if the integration constraint is slack at $w = w_2^A$, the price that solves (8), say w^F (the superscript 'F' for "forbidden"), must exceed w_2^A.[19] Assuming that welfare (measured as the sum of consumer and producer surplus) is decreasing in the wholesale price, we have the following proposition.

---

[19]This follows from the strict quasi-concavity of the Nash product ϕ_2, Assumption 2.

15

Proposition 1 *Suppose that when price discrimination is allowed, the integration constraint is slack. If downstream firms are symmetric, and if there is no integration under either regime, the wholesale price is lower and welfare is higher when price discrimination is practiced than when it is forbidden.*

The intuition for this result can be seen by rewriting condition (8) when the integration constraint is slack as

$$(10) \qquad \frac{\gamma_2[(-\partial\pi_2/\partial w_2) + (-\partial\pi_2/\partial w_1)]}{\pi_2 - d_2} = \frac{(1-\gamma_2)[(\partial U/\partial w_2) + (\partial U/\partial w_1)]}{U - d_{u2}}.$$

Notice that this condition is the same as condition (6) except that firm 2's concession cost is lower by $\partial\pi_2/\partial w_1$ and the supplier's concession cost is higher by $\partial U/\partial w_1$. A policy forbidding price discrimination reduces firm 2's concession cost because an agreement to pay a higher price requires its rival to pay a higher price too. On the other hand, the policy increases the supplier's concession cost because an agreement to charge a lower price must be granted to firm 1 as well as firm 2. Both concession cost effects strengthen the supplier's relative bargaining position, allowing it to negotiate a higher wholesale price.

Next, suppose that the chain has greater bargaining power than the independent and that the supplier still negotiates the common price with the independent. The bargaining equilibrium when discrimination is allowed is represented by point A^1 in Figure 2, where wholesale prices are $(w_1^{A^1}, w_2^{A^1})$. The effects of forbidding price discrimination can be seen by evaluating condition (8) at the wholesale prices that *would be* chosen when discrimination is allowed *if* the chain's bargaining power were the same as the independent's. This is point A^0 in Figure 2, where wholesale prices are (w^{A^0}, w^{A^0}). Since this price lies on the independent's bargaining reaction function, it must be true that $\partial\phi_2(w^{A^0}, w^{A^0})/\partial w_2 = 0$. Since the terms in curly braces in (8) are positive and the Nash product is strictly quasi-concave, this implies that the wholesale price that solves (8), w^F, exceeds w^{A^0}.

16

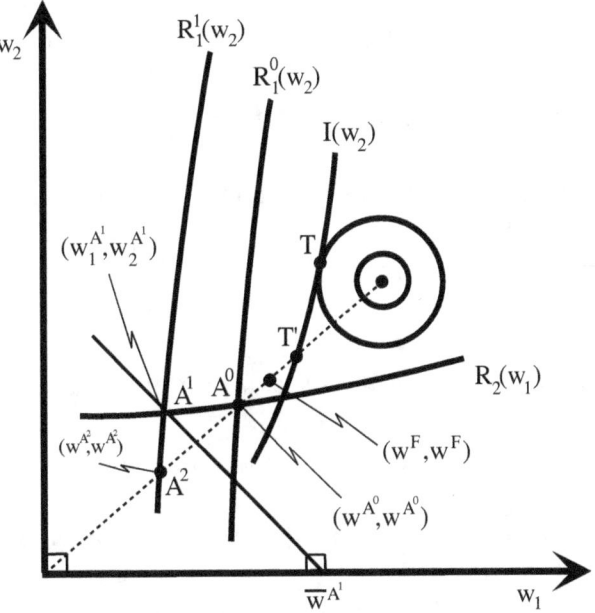

Figure 2: Wholesale price effects of forbidding price discrimination.

Consider the line through point A^1 with a slope of negative one. The average wholesale price is constant along this line and is given by $\overline{w}^{A^1} = (w_1^{A^1} + w_2^{A^2})/2$. By Lemma 1, A^0 lies above and to the right of this line. Since $w^F > w^{A^0}$, it follows that forbidding price discrimination raises the average wholesale price. Note that the supplier's profits are increasing in the average wholesale price by the assumption that U is strictly quasi-concave. Note further that if the chain were the weaker firm, and if the supplier negotiated the common price with the chain, the same argument would hold with the subscripts reversed. Therefore, if the supplier can select the downstream firm that will negotiate the wholesale price, the average wholesale price will be higher when discrimination is forbidden than when it is practiced.

Proposition 2 *Suppose that when price discrimination is allowed, the integration constraint is slack, and that the supplier can select which downstream firm will negotiate the common price. Then if there is no integration under either regime, the average wholesale price is higher when discrimination is practiced than when it is forbidden.*

Augustin Cournot (1838) has shown that the Cournot equilibrium output is decreasing in the average marginal cost of the Cournot competitors. If downstream firms produce under the same fixed proportions technology, welfare is an increasing function of the total output. These observations yield the following corollary to Proposition 2 for the case of Cournot competition in the downstream market.

Corollary 1 *Suppose that when price discrimination is allowed, the integration constraint is slack, and that the supplier can select which downstream firm will negotiate the common price. Suppose further that downstream firms are Cournot competitors that employ a fixed proportions technology. Then if there is no integration under either regime, total output and welfare are higher when price discrimination is practiced than when it is forbidden.*

Katz's Proposition 1 shows that in the take-it or leave-it environment, if integration occurs in neither regime, output and welfare are lower when price discrimination is practiced than when it is forbidden. Propositions 1 and 2 (and Corollary 1) above show that this result is reversed if three conditions hold: i) downstream firms have bargaining power from sources other than outside options; ii) the chain integration threat is not credible (i.e., the constraint is slack) when price discrimination is allowed; and iii) downstream firms are symmetric, *or* the supplier can select which downstream firm will negotiate a common price. The results of the take-it or leave-it and bargaining environments can be compared using Figure 2. In the take-it or leave-it environment, a policy forbidding price discrimination causes the supplier to reduce wholesale prices from T to T'. Intuitively, a reduction in the independent's wholesale price to bring it in line with the chain's price reduces the chain's profits, requiring a reduction in the chain's wholesale price to prevent it from integrating backward. Thus, *both* wholesale prices fall when discrimination is forbidden.[20] This result relies on the chain having a credible

---

[20]Katz also considered a case in which the chain's integration incentives are increasing in the price w_2

threat to integrate backward at the prices offered by the supplier in both regimes, so that a prohibition on price discrimination causes the supplier to adjust prices along the chain integration constraint $I(w_2)$. If the integration constraint is slack when discrimination is allowed, this effect is absent. The policy still affects concession costs, however, in a way that increases the supplier's relative bargaining power with either downstream firm. Under the conditions of Propositions 1 and 2, this effect causes both wholesale prices to rise.

The next case to consider arises when firms are asymmetric and the supplier negotiates a common price with the stronger buyer, assumed to be the chain. This might occur if downstream firms could coordinate on the order in which they bargain, or if the supplier is better off accepting the chain's terms than either risking a lawsuit for engaging in price discrimination or selling only to the independent. A diagrammatic argument similar to the one above suggests that the effects of forbidding price discrimination are generally ambiguous in this case. To see this, suppose that point A^1 in Figure 2 represents the equilibrium wholesale prices when discrimination is allowed. If the independent had bargaining power as high as the chain's, the equilibrium price would be point A^2. By arguments similar to those made above, the supplier and the chain will negotiate a common price greater than w^{A^2}, but this price may or may not exceed $\overline{w}^{A^1}$. If the chain has only a little more bargaining power than the independent (i.e., if R_1^1 is close to R_1^0), then $w^F > \overline{w}^{A^1}$.[21] But if the chain's bargaining power exceeds the independent's by a large amount, (R_1^1 well to the left of R_1^0), then it is possible that $w^F < \overline{w}^{A^1}$.[22]

---

offered by the supplier to the independent. This can arise in his model if a higher value of w_2 signals that the supplier has higher costs and would charge a higher price to the independent after chain integration. In this case, the integration constraint is downward sloping. A policy forbidding price discrimination can result in a higher wholesale price for the chain, but it still causes the average wholesale price to fall in his model if the chain chooses non-integration in both regimes.

[21] This follows from the continuity of the equilibrium prices in the parameters that affect bargaining power.

[22] The effects of forbidding price discrimination in my model have an analogy with "pattern bargaining" in union-labor negotiations. Under pattern bargaining, the labor union negotiates wage rates with one firm and then offers them on a take-it or leave-it basis to the other. Paul W. Dobson (1994) examined the circumstances under which unions prefer pattern bargaining over simultaneous negotiations with downstream Cournot competitors who face linear demand. He shows that the union gains by negotiating with the firm

To get an idea of the degree of asymmetry required for a policy against price discrimination to be beneficial when the stronger buyer conducts the bargaining, I have solved an example with Cournot competition in the downstream market. The inverse demand is $P(X) = 1 - X$ where X is aggregate output, the supplier's marginal cost is $c = 0$, and $\gamma_1 = \gamma_2 = 1/2$.[23] In the example, I varied d_1, d_2, d_{u1}, and d_{u2} over a four dimensional grid such that Assumptions 1–4 are satisfied and profitable equilibria without integration exist.[24] The results are presented in Figure 3. In this example, the smallest chain discount such

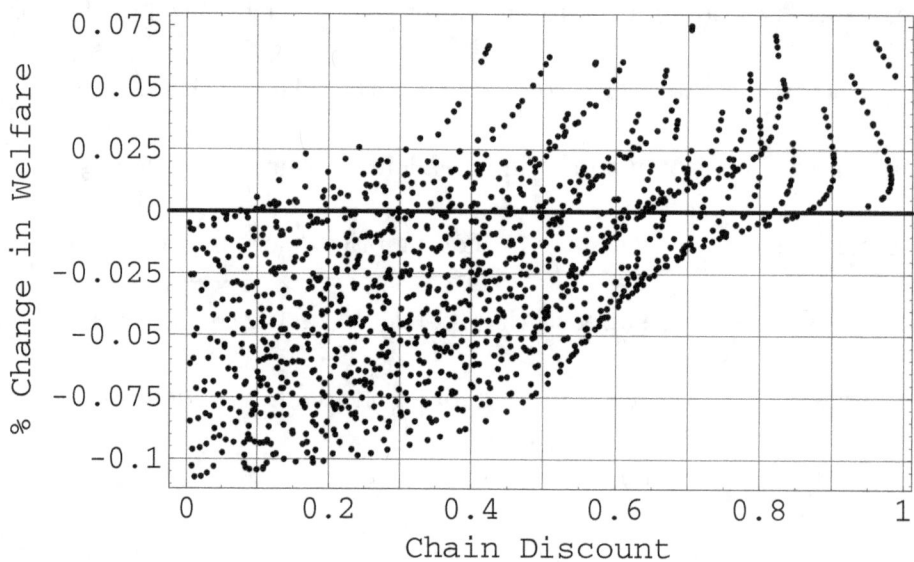

Figure 3: Welfare effects of forbidding price discrimination for different values of the discount negotiated by the chain when discrimination is allowed.

that a policy forbidding price discrimination increases welfare is 7.7 percent. The welfare

---

that is in the weaker bargaining position. My analysis differs from his in three main respects. First, I consider how the potential for backward integration and inside and outside options affect different sources of bargaining power, and how each source is affected by a policy forbidding price discrimination. Second, I focus on the welfare effects of forbidding price discrimination. Third, I allow for more general rivalry in the downstream market, and consider how the effects of forbidding price discrimination vary with the nature of downstream rivalry (section IV below).

[23]The Cournot equilibrium output of firm i is $x_i(w_1, w_2) = (1 - 2w_i + w_2)/3$, $i \in \{1, 2\}$, and total output is $X(w_1, w_2) = x_1(w_1, w_2) + x_2(w_1, w_2)$. The firms' profits are $\pi_i(w_1, w_2) = (1 - 2w_i + w_j)^2/9$, $i \in \{1, 2\}$, and $U(w_1, w_2) = (w_1 - c)x_1(w_1, w_2) + (w_2 - c)x_2(w_1, w_2)$.

[24]In this example the joint monopoly profit is 0.25. Varying the supplier's disagreement profits from 0 to 0.14 and the buyers' disagreement profits from 0 to 0.15 was sufficient to cover the relevant part of the grid. I varied d_{u1} and d_{u2} in increments of 0.02 and d_1 and d_2 in increments of 0.01.

benefits of forbidding price discrimination, when they exist, tend to be small (less than 3 percent if the chain discount is less than 30 percent.) The welfare cost of forbidding price discrimination can be as high as about 10 percent even when the chain negotiates discounts as high as 25 percent.

IV.   Two Special Cases

Equations (6) and (10) are useful for motivating how the results are affected by different assumptions about downstream rivalry. Suppose that firms 1 and 2 are monopolists in different markets. In this case $\partial \pi_2 / \partial w_1 = 0$ because the downstream firms do not compete. A policy forbidding price discrimination therefore does not affect the downstream firms' concession costs, but it still increases the supplier's concession costs (e.g., by $\partial U / \partial w_1$ in negotiations with firm 2), leading to a higher wholesale price.[25]

The presence of downstream competition reinforces the concession cost effect of forbidding price discrimination because the policy then affects downstream firms' concession costs. A natural question is whether this bargaining effect persists as downstream rivalry becomes more intense. Intuitively, one might think that as the downstream market becomes more competitive, each downstream firm's bargaining power would fall. If the supplier had all the bargaining power in both regimes, the bargaining model would collapse to the take-it or leave-it model. This intuition turns out to be incorrect. In fact, the wholesale price effects of forbidding price discrimination can get worse as downstream rivalry becomes more intense.

To demonstrate this point, I consider an example in which downstream firms sell homogeneous products and engage in rivalry that can be summarized by the following pricing

---

[25]This result is similar to the finding of Cooper and Fries (1993) that most-favored-nation pricing by a monopolist to independent buyers can lead to higher prices when prices are negotiated. Cooper and Fries did not consider the case of competing downstream firms, asymmetric bargaining powers, or the potential for backward integration.

rule:

$$(11) \qquad P(X) = w_i - \theta P'(X)x_i, \quad i \in \{1, 2\}$$

where X is industry output, $P(X)$ is the inverse demand, x_i is firm i's output, and $\theta \in [0, 2]$ is a parameter that measures industry conduct.[26] I assume that the industry revenue function, $R(X) = P(X)X$, is concave. The solution to the two equations in (11) yields downstream equilibrium quantities x_1^θ and x_2^θ. As θ falls, rivalry becomes more intense in the sense that price falls toward marginal cost. The Cournot outcome occurs when $\theta = 1$. If $w_1 = w_2$, the monopoly outcome occurs when $\theta = 2$, and the competitive outcome arises when $\theta = 0$.

Denote the reduced form profits the same way as in previous sections, but with the superscript θ to indicate their dependence on downstream conduct. Firm i's equilibrium profits are $\pi_i^\theta = (P - w_i)x_i^\theta$, $i \in \{1, 2\}$, and the supplier's profits are $U^\theta = (w_1 - c)x_1^\theta + (w_2 - c)x_2^\theta$. If the integration constraint is slack, the equilibrium wholesale prices when price discrimination is allowed solve

$$(12) \qquad \frac{\gamma_i[-\partial \pi_i^\theta / \partial w_i]}{\pi_i^\theta - d_i} = \frac{(1 - \gamma_i)[\partial U^\theta / \partial w_i]}{U^\theta - d_{ui}}, \quad i \in \{1, 2\}.$$

Assuming symmetry, the equilibrium wholesale price when price discrimination is forbidden solves

$$(13) \quad \frac{\gamma_i[(-\partial \pi_i^\theta / \partial w_i) + (-\partial \pi_i^\theta / \partial w_j)]}{\pi_i^\theta - d_i} = \frac{(1 - \gamma_i)[\partial U^\theta / \partial w_i + \partial U^\theta / \partial w_j]}{U^\theta - d_{ui}}, \quad i \in \{1, 2\}, \ i \neq j.$$

Straightforward comparative statics show that for all $\theta \in (0, 2]$, $\partial U^\theta / \partial w_i > 0$, $\partial \pi_i^\theta / \partial w_i < 0$, and $\partial \pi_i / \partial w_j > 0$ over the range of conflict. Thus, if Assumptions 1–4 hold, and if net profits are positive, Lemma 1 and Proposition 1 go through. The effect of more intense rivalry on bargaining equilibria in the two regimes depends on how the firms' reduced-form profits and concession costs vary with θ. The derivative of these expressions with respect to θ depends

---

[26]This rule is familiar from empirical applications in the "New Empirical IO" (NEIO) tradition, which interpret θ as a measure of industry conduct. See, for example, Timothy F. Bresnahan (1989), David Genesove and Wallace P. Mullin (1998) and Catherine Wolfram (1999).

on the third derivative of the inverse demand function and hence cannot be signed without further assumptions. However, it is possible to determine the values of profits and concession costs under symmetry in the limit as $\theta \to 0$.

Lemma 2 *Suppose $w_1 = w_2 = w$. Then the following conditions hold in the limit as the downstream market becomes competitive:*

$$(14) \qquad \lim_{\theta \to 0} \left(\frac{\partial U^\theta}{\partial w_i} \right) = x_i^\theta + \frac{w - c}{2P'(X^\theta)},$$

$$(15) \qquad \lim_{\theta \to 0} \left(-\frac{\partial \pi^\theta}{\partial w_i} \right) = \frac{x_i^\theta}{2},$$

$$(16) \qquad \lim_{\theta \to 0} \pi_i^\theta = 0.$$

$$(17) \qquad \lim_{\theta \to 0} \left(-\frac{\partial \pi_i^\theta}{\partial w_i} - \frac{\partial \pi_i^\theta}{\partial w_j} \right) = -\frac{P''(X^\theta)X^\theta + P'(X^\theta)}{(P'(X^\theta))^2 \, X^\theta}$$

Conditions (14) and (15) show that when price discrimination is allowed, the concession costs of the supplier and downstream firm i are bounded and have the expected signs ($\partial U^\theta / \partial w_i > 0$ for small enough w and $-\partial \pi_i^\theta / \partial w_i > 0$) in the limit as the downstream market becomes *perfectly* competitive. Condition (16) shows that downstream firms' profits go to zero as the market becomes competitive, as expected. Thus, downstream firm i's concession costs as a percentage of its gains from trade rise to infinity as the downstream market becomes competitive. Since the percentage concession costs of firm i and the supplier must be equalized in a bargaining equilibrium, the supplier's percentage concession costs must also rise to infinity, which requires its net profits to fall to zero too. This establishes the following proposition.

Proposition 3 *Suppose that downstream firms are symmetric. In a bargaining equilibrium when price discrimination is allowed, the supplier's net profits fall to zero as the downstream market becomes perfectly competitive.*

23

This result may seem counter-intuitive at first, but it has a natural interpretation in a bargaining environment. A firm's bargaining power comes partly from its ability to inflict a loss on the firm it is negotiating with by delaying an agreement. When the downstream market is highly competitive, downstream firms earn little profit, so the supplier inflicts only a small loss on each firm by delaying an agreement. The "inflicted loss" source of the supplier's bargaining power falls to zero as the downstream market becomes perfectly competitive, so that in the limit as $\theta \to 0$ the supplier does no better than earning its disagreement profits.

Next, consider the effects of forbidding price discrimination as the downstream market becomes competitive. Condition (17) in Lemma 2 implies that when price discrimination is forbidden, firm i's concession costs as a percentage of its net profits are positive and finite (using the assumption that $R(X)$ is concave). From condition (13), the supplier's percentage concession costs must also be positive and finite, which requires $U^\theta - d_{ui} > 0$. Thus, as the downstream market becomes more competitive, wholesale prices remain higher when price discrimination is forbidden than when it is allowed.

Proposition 4 *Suppose that downstream firms are symmetric, and that downstream rivalry is described by the conduct parameter θ in condition (11). For all $\theta \in [0, 2]$, total output and welfare are lower when price discrimination is forbidden than when it is practiced.*

Figure 4 plots the equilibrium wholesale price and welfare as a function of θ for an example in which $P(X) = 1 - X$, $c = 0$, $\lambda_1 = \lambda_2 = 1/2$, $d_1 = d_2 = 0$, and $d_{u1} = d_{u2} = 3/32$.[27] In this example, a policy forbidding price discrimination has a larger effect on wholesale prices the more competitive the market, as measured by the conduct parameter. Welfare rises as the market becomes more competitive in both regimes, but the percentage reduction in welfare

---

[27]The supplier's profit under successive monopoly is 3/32.

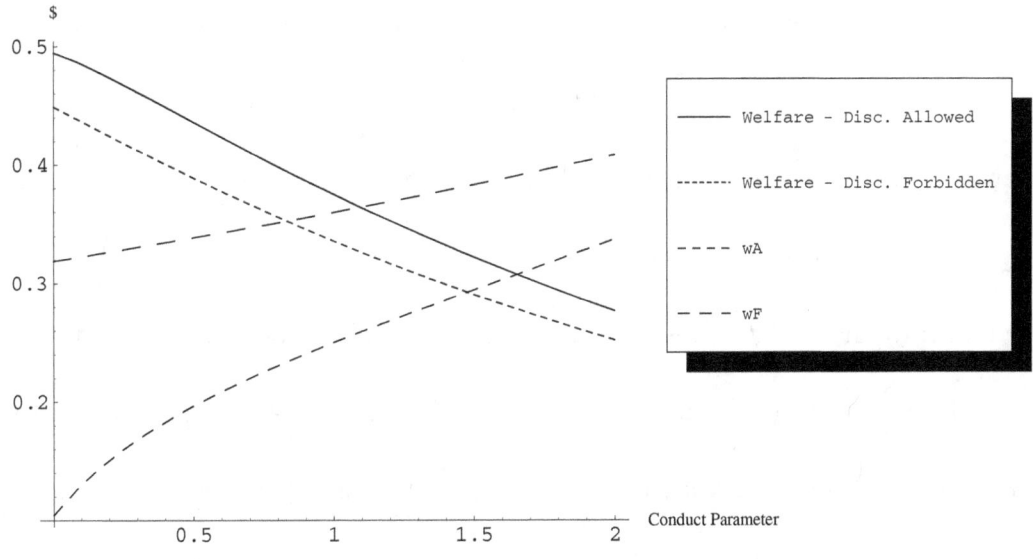

Figure 4: Wholesale prices and welfare as functions of the conduct parameter.

from a policy forbidding price discrimination remains roughly constant at about 10 percent.

V. Conclusion

The main implication of this paper is that the welfare effects of forbidding price discrimination in intermediate good markets turn partly on the source of the bargaining power used by downstream firms to extract discounts. Katz's results imply that if discounts are extracted by explicit threats to integrate backward, then forbidding price discrimination can be socially beneficial. My results show that if the discounts are derived from some other source of bargaining power, e.g., a greater disagreement profit for the chain, or a greater bargaining weight, then forbidding price discrimination is often socially harmful.

The passage of the Robinson-Patman Act provides an experiment that in principle might allow one to distinguish between the bargaining and take-it or leave-it models in different industries. Where discounts arose from credible threats to integrate backward, both models predict that the average wholesale price would have fallen after Robinson-Patman was passed

25

if the supplier adjusted wholesale prices to prevent chain integration. The law would have made the supplier worse off in such markets. Where discounts arose from other sources of bargaining power, the model predicts that the average wholesale price could have risen after the law was passed. The supplier could have benefited from the law in such markets.

A formal study of the effects of the Robinson-Patman Act on prices has not been conducted, to my knowledge. However, the effects of Robinson-Patman on profits have been explored both informally and using econometric methods. Morris Adelman (1959) conducted an informal study of the wholesale pricing and purchasing practices of A&P, the dominant grocery chain of the 1920s and 1930s. He argues that that suppliers with strong brand positions that sold to A&P benefited from the Robinson-Patman Act.[28] This conclusion is consistent with chain bargaining power arising from concession costs, disagreement profits, and bargaining weights. It is not consistent with the predictions of the take-it or leave-it model.[29]

The most comprehensive formal study is that of Thomas W. Ross (1984). He used event study methodology to evaluate the abnormal returns of grocery chains and manufacturers after the Robinson-Patman Act was passed and after various enforcement actions were undertaken by the U.S. Federal Trade Commission (FTC). He found that the stock market values of the major grocery chains in the U.S. fell significantly after the Act was passed. This conclusion is consistent with the predictions of the bargaining model. It is not consistent with the take-it or leave-it model, which predicts that the chain firm's profits should equal the expected value of its outside option whether price discrimination is allowed or forbidden.[30]

---

[28] See Adelman, p. 190.

[29] Adelman's conclusion would also be consistent with the view that the Robinson-Patman Act facilitates collusion among suppliers. However, collusion among *differentiated* manufacturers with strong brand positions is notoriously difficult. Thus, the bargaining model probably provides a more plausible explanation for Adelman's conclusion.

[30] Ross was not able to reject the hypothesis that the Robinson-Patman Act had no effect on the stock

The implications of bargaining for antitrust policy are not well understood. However, bargaining is prevalent in intermediate good markets, where a large share of the antitrust enforcement in developed countries takes place. This paper shows that bargaining has important implications for understanding the effects of the Robinson-Patman Act. There is every reason to believe that bargaining could have important implications for understanding the effects of antitrust laws governing mergers, vertical restraints, and collusion as well.

---

market values of grocery manufacturers in the U.S.

APPENDIX

Proof of Lemma 1

Differentiating the system (3) and (5) when the integration constraint is slack yields

$$(18) \qquad \frac{\partial w_i^A}{\partial \gamma_i} = \frac{\frac{\partial^2 \phi_i}{\partial w_i^2} \left(\frac{\partial U}{\partial w_i}[\pi_i - d_i] - \frac{\partial \pi_i}{\partial w_i}[U - d_{ui}] \right)}{D},$$

$$(19) \qquad \frac{\partial (w_j^A - w_i^A)}{\partial \gamma_i} = \frac{-\left\{ \frac{\partial^2 \phi_i}{\partial w_i^2} + \frac{\partial^2 \phi_i}{\partial w_i \partial w_j} \right\} \left(\frac{\partial U}{\partial w_i}[\pi_i - d_i] - \frac{\partial \pi_i}{\partial w_i}[U - d_{ui}] \right)}{D},$$

$$(20) \qquad \frac{\partial w_i^A}{\partial d_i} = \frac{\frac{\partial^2 \phi_i}{\partial w_i^2} \left([1 - \gamma_i]\frac{\partial U}{\partial w_i} \right)}{D},$$

$$(21) \qquad \frac{\partial (w_j^A - w_i^A)}{\partial d_i} = \frac{-\left\{ \frac{\partial^2 \phi_i}{\partial w_i^2} + \frac{\partial^2 \phi_i}{\partial w_i \partial w_j} \right\} \left([1 - \gamma_i]\frac{\partial U}{\partial w_i} \right)}{D},$$

$$(22) \qquad \frac{\partial w_i^A}{\partial d_{ui}} = \frac{\frac{\partial^2 \phi_i}{\partial w_i^2} \left(\gamma_i \frac{\partial \pi_i}{\partial w_i} \right)}{D},$$

$$(23) \qquad \frac{\partial (w_j^A - w_i^A)}{\partial d_{ui}} = \frac{-\left\{ \frac{\partial^2 \phi_i}{\partial w_i^2} + \frac{\partial^2 \phi_i}{\partial w_i \partial w_j} \right\} \left(\gamma_i \frac{\partial \pi_i}{\partial w_i} \right)}{D},$$

where

$$(24) \qquad D = \left(\frac{\partial^2 \phi_1}{\partial w_1^2} \right) \left(\frac{\partial^2 \phi_2}{\partial w_2^2} \right) - \left(\frac{\partial^2 \phi_1}{\partial w_1 \partial w_2} \right) \left(\frac{\partial^2 \phi_2}{\partial w_2 \partial w_1} \right).$$

Note that $\partial U/\partial w_i > 0$ and $\partial \pi_i/\partial w_i < 0$ over the range of conflict, and the net profit terms $U - d_{ui}$ and $\pi_i = d_i$ are positive in equilibrium. The second derivative $\partial^2 \phi_i/\partial w_i^2$ is negative by Assumption 2. Thus, the sign of the derivatives in (18)-(23) depends on the signs of the terms in curly brackets and the sign of D. Differentiating (3) and (5) individually when the integration constraint is slack yields

$$(25) \qquad \frac{\partial^2 \phi_i}{\partial w_i \partial w_j} = -R_i'(w_j)\frac{\partial^2 \phi_i}{\partial w_i^2}.$$

Substituting (25) into (24) and using Assumptions 4 and 2 implies that $D > 0$. Substituting (24) and (25) into the derivatives (18) through (23) yields the results in the Lemma.

Proof of Lemma 2

For future reference we need the derivatives of the equilibrium quantities with respect to w_1. Differentiating the system (11) with respect to w_1 gives

$$(26) \qquad \begin{pmatrix} \Omega_{11} & \Omega_{12} \\ \Omega_{21} & \Omega_{22} \end{pmatrix} \begin{pmatrix} \partial x_1^\theta / \partial w_1 \\ \partial x_2^\theta / \partial w_1 \end{pmatrix} = \begin{pmatrix} 1 \\ 0 \end{pmatrix}$$

where $\Omega_{ii} = \theta P'' x_i + (1+\theta)P'$ and $\Omega_{ij} = \theta P'' x_i + P'$, $i \in \{1,2\}$, $i \neq j$. Let $D^\theta = \Omega_{11}\Omega_{22} - \Omega_{12}\Omega_{21} = P'[\theta^2 P'' X^\theta + \theta(2+\theta)P']$. Solving (26) gives

$$(27) \qquad \frac{\partial x_1^\theta}{\partial w_1} = \frac{\Omega_{22}}{D^\theta} = \frac{\theta P'' x_2^\theta + (1+\theta)P'}{D^\theta}$$

$$(28) \qquad \frac{\partial x_2^\theta}{\partial w_1} = \frac{-\Omega_{21}}{D^\theta} = \frac{-[\theta P'' x_2^\theta + (1+\theta)P']}{D^\theta}.$$

We can now calculate the derivatives in the Lemma and verify the limits. Differentiating the supplier's profits and evaluating at $w_1 = w_2 = w$ yields

$$(29) \qquad \frac{\partial U^\theta}{\partial w_1} = x_1^\theta + (w-c)\left(\frac{\partial x_1^\theta}{\partial w_1} + \frac{\partial x_2^\theta}{\partial w_1} \right)$$

$$(30) \qquad = x_1^\theta + \frac{(w-c)\theta}{\Delta}$$

where $\Delta = D^\theta / P' = \theta^2 P'' X^\theta + \theta(2+\theta)P'$. Let $X^{\theta'}$, and Δ' denote derivatives with respect to θ. By L'Hopital's rule,

$$(31) \qquad \lim_{\theta \to 0} \frac{\theta}{\Delta} = \lim_{\theta \to 0} \left(\frac{1}{\Delta'} \right)$$

$$(32) \qquad = \lim_{\theta \to 0} \left(\frac{1}{2\theta P'' X^\theta + \theta^2 [P''' X^\theta + P''] X^{\theta'} + 2(1+\theta)P' + \theta(2+\theta)P'' X^{\theta'}} \right)$$

$$(33) \qquad = \frac{1}{2P'}.$$

Substituting (33) into (30) and imposing symmetry yields (14).

The limit of firm 1's concession cost is

$$(34) \qquad \lim_{\theta \to 0} \left(-\frac{\partial \pi_1^\theta}{\partial w_1} \right) = \lim_{\theta \to 0} \left(-P' \left[\frac{\partial x_1^\theta}{\partial w_1} + \frac{\partial x_2^\theta}{\partial w_1} \right] x_1^\theta + x_1^\theta \right)$$

$$(35) \qquad = \lim_{\theta \to 0} \left(-\frac{P'\theta}{\Delta} x_1^\theta + x_1^\theta \right).$$

Substituting (33) into (35) and imposing symmetry yields (15).

Inspection of condition (11) implies that $P \to w_i$ as $\theta \to 0$. This implies condition (16).

Let $w_1 = w_2 = w$. Using symmetry, the limit of firm 1's concession costs when price discrimination is forbidden is

$$(36) \qquad \lim_{\theta \to 0} \left(\frac{-\left[\frac{\partial \pi_1^\theta}{\partial w_1} + \frac{\partial \pi_1^\theta}{\partial w_2} \right]}{\pi_1^\theta} \right) = \lim_{\theta \to 0} \frac{\left(-2P' \left[\frac{\partial x_1^\theta}{\partial w_1} + \frac{\partial x_2^\theta}{\partial w_1} \right] x_1^\theta + x_1^\theta \right)}{(P - w)x_1^\theta}$$

$$(37) \qquad \qquad = \lim_{\theta \to 0} \left(\frac{\theta^2 [P'' X^\theta + P']}{(P - w)\Delta} \right).$$

Both the numerator and denominator of (37) converge to zero as $\theta \to 0$. Let $A = P'' X^\theta + P'$, and let A' denote the derivative of A with respect to θ. Applying L'Hopital's rule to condition (37) twice, we have

$$(38) \; \lim_{\theta \to 0} \left(\frac{\theta^2 [P'' X^\theta + P']}{(P - w)\Delta} \right) = \lim_{\theta \to 0} \left(\frac{2\theta A + \theta^2 A'}{P' X^{\theta'} \Delta + (P - w)\Delta'} \right)$$

$$(39) \qquad \qquad = \lim_{\theta \to 0} \left(\frac{2A + 4\theta A' + \theta^2 A''}{[P''(X^{\theta'})^2 + P' X^{\theta''}]\Delta + 2\Delta' P' X^{\theta'} + (P - w)\Delta''} \right)$$

$$(40) \qquad \qquad = \lim_{\theta \to 0} \left(\frac{2A}{2\Delta' P' X^{\theta'}} \right).$$

The derivative of Δ is

$$(41) \qquad \Delta' = 2\theta P'' X^\theta + \theta^2 [P''' X^\theta + P''] X^{\theta'} + (2 + 2\theta)P' + \theta(2 + \theta)P'' X^{\theta'}$$

Taking the limit gives

$$(42) \qquad \qquad \lim_{\theta \to 0} \Delta' = 2P'.$$

The derivative of X^θ is found by differentiating (11) with respect to θ and imposing symmetry. This gives

$$(43) \qquad \qquad X^{\theta'} = \frac{-P' X^\theta}{\theta P'' X^\theta + (2 + \theta)P'}$$

and

$$(44) \qquad \qquad \lim_{\theta \to 0} X^{\theta'} = \frac{-X^\theta}{2}.$$

Condition (17) results from substituting conditions (42) and (44) into (40).

REFERENCES

Adelman, M.A. *A & P: A Study in Price-Cost Behavior and Public Policy.* Cambridge: Harvard University Press, 1959.

Areeda, Phillip and Kaplow, Louis. *Antitrust Analysis: Problems, Text, Cases.* Boston: Little, Brown and Company, 1988.

Binmore, Ken and Dasgupta, Partha. "Nash Bargaining Theory: An Introduction," in Ken Binmore and Partha Dasgupta, ed., *The Economics of Bargaining.* New York: Basil Blackwell, 1987.

Binmore, Ken, Rubinstein, Ariel and Wolinsky, Asher. "The Nash Bargaining Solution in Economic Modelling." *Rand Journal of Economics*, Summer 1986, 17, pp. 176-88.

Bresnahan, Timothy F. "Empirical Studies of Industries with Market Power," in Richard Schmalensee and Robert D. Willig, ed., *Handbook of Industrial Organization*, vol. 2. New York: North Holland, 1989.

Carlton, Dennis W. and Perloff, Jeffrey M. *Modern Industrial Organization.* New York: Harper Collins, 1994.

Cooper, Thomas E. and Fries, Timothy L. "The Most-Favored-Nation Pricing Policy and Negotiated Prices." *International Journal of Industrial Organization*, 9(2), 1991, pp. 209-23.

DeGraba, Patrick. "Input Market Price Discrimination and the Choice of Technology." *American Economic Review*, December 1990, 80(5), pp. 1246-53.

DeGraba, Patrick, and Postlewaite, Andrew. "Exclusivity Clauses and Best Price Policies in Input Markets," *Journal of Economics and Management Strategy.* Fall 1992, 1(3), pp. 423-54.

DeGraba, Patrick. "Most-Favored-Customer Clauses and Multilateral Contracting: When Nondiscrimination Implies Uniformity." *Journal of Economics and Management Strategy*, Winter 1996, 5(4), pp. 565-79.

Dobson, Paul. "Multifirm Unions and the Incentive to Adopt Pattern Bargaining in Oligopoly." *European Economic Review*, January 1994, 38(1), pp. 87-100.

Gallet, Craig A. "Public Policy and Market Power in the Rayon Industry." *Journal of Economics and Business*, 1997, 49 pp. 369-377.

Genesove, David and Mullin, Wallace P. "Testing Static Oligopoly Models:Conduct and Cost in the Sugar Industry, 1890-1914." *Rand Journal of Economics*, Summer 1998, 29(2), pp. 355-77.

Harsanyi, John C. "Approaches to the Bargaining Problem Before and After the Theory of Games: A Critical Discussion of Zeuthen's, Hicks', and Nash's Theories." *Econometrica*, April 1956, 24(2), pp. 144-57.

Katz, Michael L. "The Welfare Effects of Third-Degree Price Discrimination in Intermediate Goods Markets." *American Economic Review*, March 1987, 77(1) pp. 154-67.

Malueg, David A. "Bounding the Welfare Effects of Third-Degree Price Discrimination." *American Economic Review*, September 1993, 83(4), pp. 1011-21.

McAfee, R. Preston and Schwartz, Marius. "Opportunism in Multilateral Vertical Contracting: Nondiscrimination, Exclusivity, and Uniformity." *American Economic Review*, March 1994, 84(1), pp. 210-30.

Muthoo, Abhinay. *Bargaining Theory with Applications.* Cambridge: Cambridge University Press, 1999.

Nash, John F. "The Bargaining Problem." *Econometrica*, 1950, 18, pp. 155-62.

O'Brien, Daniel P. and Shaffer Greg. "The Welfare Effects of Forbidding Discriminatory Discounts: A Secondary Line Analysis of Robinson-Patman." *Journal of Law, Economics, and Organization*, October 1994, 10(2), pp. 296-318.

Pigou, A.C. *The Economics of Welfare.* London: Macmillan, 1932.

Robinson, Joan. *The Economics of Imperfect Competition.* London: MacMillen, 1933.

Ross, Thomas W. "Winners and Losers Under the Robinson-Patman Act." *Journal of Law and Economics*, October 1984, 27, pp. 243-271.

Rubinstein, Ariel. "Perfect Equilibrium in a Bargaining Model." *Econometrica*, 50, pp. 97-110.

Schmalensee, Richard. "Output and Welfare Implications of Monopolistic Third-Degree Price Discrimination." *American Economic Review*, March 1981, 71, pp. 242-47.

Schwartz, Marius. "The Perverse Effects of the Robinson-Patman Act." *Antitrust Bulletin*, Fall 1986, 31(3), pp. 733-57.

Schwartz, Marius. "Third Degree Price Discrimination and Output: Generalizing a Welfare Result." *American Economic Review*, December 1990, 80(5), pp. 1259-62.

Shaked, Avner and John Sutton. "Involuntary Unemployment as a Perfect Equilibrium in a Bargaining Model," *Econometrica* 52, pp. 1351-1364.

Snyder, Christopher M. "A Dynamic Theory of Countervailing Power." *Rand Journal of Economics*, Winter 1996, 27(4), pp.747-69.

Varian, Hal. "Price Discrimination and Social Welfare." *American Economic Review*, September 1985, 75, pp. 870-75.

Wolfram, Catherine D. "Measuring Duopoly Power in the British Electricity Spot Market." *American Economic Review*, September 1999, 89(4), pp. 805-26.

Yoshida, Yoshihiro. "Third-Degree Price Discrimination in Input Markets: Output and Welfare." *American Economic Review*, March 2000, 90(1), pp. 240-46.

Zeuthen, Frederik. *Problems of Monopoly and Economic Warfare.* London: George Routledge and Sons, 1930.